GW00771443

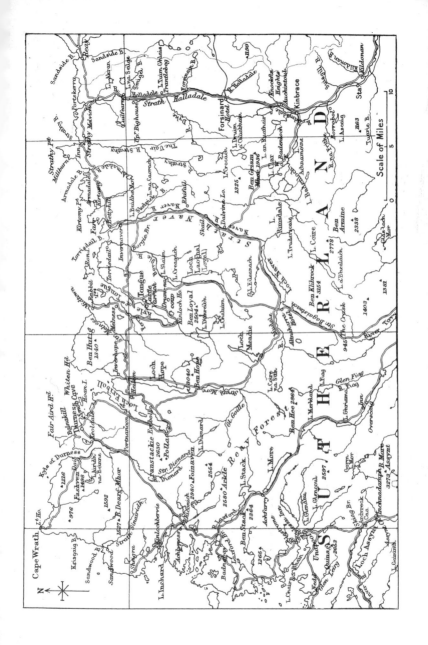

PERSONAL ARMS OF LORD REAY,
CHIEF OF CLAN MACKAY

JOHNSTON'S CLAN HISTORIES

THE CLAN MACKAY

Clansman's Badge

JOHNSTON'S CLAN HISTORIES

THE CLAN CAMERON. BY C.I. FRASER OF REELIG, *Sometime Albany Herald*.

THE CLAN CAMPBELL. BY ANDREW MCKERRAL, C.I.E.

THE CLAN DONALD. (Macdonald, Macdonell, Macalister). BY I.F GRANT, LL.D.

THE FERGUSSONS. BY SIR JAMES FERGUSSON OF KILKERRAN, BT.

THE CLAN FRASER OF LOVAT. BY C.I. FRASER OF REELIG, *Sometime Albany Herald*.

THE CLAN GORDON. BY JEAN DUNLOP, PH.D.

THE GRAHAMS. BY JOHN STEWART OF ARDVORLICH.

THE CLAN GRANT. BY I.F. GRANT, LL.D.

THE KENNEDYS. BY SIR JAMES FERGUSSON OF KILKERRAN, BT.

THE CLAN MACGREGOR. BY W.R. KERMACK.

THE CLAN MACKAY. BY MARGARET O. MACDOUGALL.

THE CLAN MACKENZIE. BY JEAN DUNLOP, PH.D.

THE CLAN MACKINTOSH. BY JEAN DUNLOP, PH.D.

THE CLAN MACLEAN. BY JOHN MACKECHNIE.

THE CLAN MACLEOD. BY I.F. GRANT, LL.D.

THE CLAN MACRAE. BY DONALD MACRAE.

THE CLAN MORRISON. BY ALICK MORRISON.

THE CLAN MUNRO. BY C.I. FRASER OF REELIG, *Sometime Albany Herald*.

THE ROBERTSONS. BY SIR IAIN MONCREIFFE OF THAT ILK, BT. *Albany Herald*.

THE CLAN ROSS. BY DONALD MACKINNON, D.LITT.

THE SCOTTS. BY JEAN DUNLOP, PH.D.

THE STEWARTS. BY JOHN STEWART OF ARDVORLICH.

THE CLAN MACKAY

A CELTIC RESISTANCE TO FEUDAL SUPERIORITY

BY

MARGARET O. MACDOUGALL,

F.S.A. Scot.

Late Librarian, Inverness Public Library

With Tartan and Chief's Arms in Colour, and a Map

JOHNSTON & BACON PUBLISHERS

EDINBURGH AND LONDON

FIRST PUBLISHED 1953
SECOND EDITION 1963
REPRINTED 1969
REPRINTED 1972

SBN 7179 4529 4

© *Johnston & Bacon Publishers*

PRINTED IN GREAT BRITAIN BY
LOWE AND BRYDONE (PRINTERS) LIMITED, LONDON

I

Duthaich Mhic Aoidh, familiarly known as the Mackay country, covered approximately five-eighths of the County of Sutherland. Measuring some eighty miles in length, it extended from Drumholstein in the east to Cape Wrath in the west, thence southward to Eddrachillis Bay which separated it from Assynt. It adjoined the lands of the Gunns, Sinclairs, Sutherlands, and MacLeods of Assynt.

In earlier times the Mackay chiefs were described as " of Strathnaver," and this term was commonly used to describe the whole Mackay country. The name " Lord Reay's Country " appears to have come into use following the year 1628 when Sir Donald Mackay of Farr was raised to the Scottish peerage as Lord Reay.

The first Mackay lands, twelve davochs of church lands at Durness, were acquired in the early thirteenth century. From this first foothold, which was secured before the Norsemen were expelled from Scotland, successive Mackay chiefs added to their estates until by the seventeenth century they owned the greater part of the modern County of Sutherland.

In 1415, the Lord of the Isles gave Angus Du Mackay, his brother-in-law, a charter on the lands of Strathhalladale and Ferrincoskry (Skibo, Creich, etc.). In the charter Angus Du is described as " of Strathnaver " (*de Strathnawir*) which suggests that the Mackays had acquired other lands in addition to the church lands at Durness. In 1499, the lands of Farr, Strathy, Armadale, Cattach, and others were given to Odo Mackay by King James IV. These lands, the confiscated possessions of Sutherland of Dirled, were Mackay's reward for capturing Dirled who had been outlawed. A royal gift of non-entry (see p. 32) in 1504 confirmed to Y Mackay all his possessions in *Duthaich Mhic Aoidh*. The islands of Strathnaver with Melness and Hope were added by purchase, Melness and Hope in 1511, and the Islands of Strathnaver in 1624. These lands had originally been gifted in 1379 to Ferchard Mackay by the Wolf of Badenoch, son of King Robert II. Ferchard was described in his charters as " the king's physician " and " the leech." He was the son of Iye Mackay killed at Dingwall in 1370. In Farr churchyard there is a beautiful sculptured stone called *Clach Fhearchar* which was traditionally said to mark the grave of Ferchard " the leech." This, however, is extremely unlikely.

In 1624 the Mackay lands reached their greatest extent, extending from the hill of Skaill to Glencoul, near Assynt, a stretch of one hundred miles. The 1st Lord Reay added considerably to his possessions by purchasing lands in Caithness from Lord Forbes.

It is a wild and rugged country of high mountains, fertile valleys, and open moorland, with rivers and lochs offering excellent fishing. The Laxford has always been regarded as the best salmon river and its name, of Norse derivation, means " the salmon ford." Other good salmon rivers are the Borgy, Hope, Dionard, and the Naver, while the whole of the Mackay country abounds in lochs full of trout. The Reay Forest, from Ben Loyal to Ben Leod, has long been famous, and many early accounts speak of the great herds of deer which roamed the forest and of the many hunting expeditions of Mackay and his guests. The country was rich in natural food. Sea fish were plentiful on the coast, trout and salmon, venison and game were all in good supply. The people raised cattle, sheep, and goats, selling the surplus not required for their own use to the markets of the south. Their crops were mainly barley, oats, and rye ; potatoes and vegetables not being cultivated until a fairly late date. They were almost self-supporting and independent of outside supplies. The facile pen of the Rev. James Fraser, author of the *Wardlaw Manuscript*, records a vivid picture of Lord Lovat's visit to Lord Reay in 1669, in the following words : " The Lord Ray contrived all manner of sport and recreation to divert his dear Lovat, as he tearmd him ; sometimes out at sea in berges afishing, sometimes haukeing and hunting, sometimes arching at buts and bowmarks, jumping, wrestling, dancing—for my Lord had his trumpeter, Hans Adam, and his expert fidler, Hugh Chisholm, with him. At last, the season approaching, they went to the hills. All the gentlemen of the name of M'kay conveend, and so to the deer hunting, for my Lord Ray hath the finest and richest forest in the kingdom for deer and reas, their number and nimbleness ; and some of them thought their luck was singular, becaus Lovat was there, and highlanders observe that short lived men have great luck of venison ; and alas ! so it appeared, for (he) lived short after this. My Lord Lovat, haveing stayed a whole month and more in Strathnaver, and, we may say, wearied with excess of pleasure, thinks of returning home the beginning of September, loadned with curtesies and obligations. My Lord Ray gifted him a curious, curled, black, shelty horse, severall excellent firelocks, bowes, and a sword that perhaps for goodness and antiquity might be called the nonsuch, and two deer greyhounds. My Lady gifted him a plaid all of silk, party colloured, her own work, and a pare of truse of the same, neatly knit, and a dublet of needlework, all which might be a present for the High Commissioner his Grace, and would needs see all these garbs put on, and in a droll called Lovat her Joseph with a coat of many collours." As in other Highland districts, the womenfolk spun and wove cloth and tartan, and from the above it is seen that Lady Reay was also accomplished in the art of making a " party colloured " plaid.

Strathnaver was the most fertile valley and the most populous. Stretching from Bettyhill to Mudale, it was from here that the greatest number of people were evicted during the Sutherland clearances. Strathnaver was the home of the Aberach Mackays, descendants of the famous Ian Aberach, leader and victor of the clan at the famous battle of Drum na coup fought near Tongue in 1433. Ian Aberach was brought up in Lochaber, his mother being a daughter of the famous Alasdair Carrach, Chief of the MacDonalds of Keppoch. He led the clan during the years when his brother Neil (Neil Vass) was a hostage on the Bass Rock.

Strathhalladale, Strathmore—birthplace of Rob Donn, Dalacharn—called " Lord Reay's dairy," Kinloch, Lettermore, and Strath Dionard are good fertile areas. Apart from the Straths there are good stretches of arable land on the coast at Reay, Melvich, Farr, Tongue, Melness, Durness, Sandwood, and Scourie. It was at Melness that Captain George Mackay and eighty men captured the crew of the *Hazard* and the treasure of £12,000 which had been sent from France to the Jacobite army in 1746. Prisoners and money were sent south on board the man-of-war *Sheerness*. The coast is rugged with beautiful sandy beaches and bays. After the clearances many families settled on the coast and carried on fishing, but lack of harbours and other circumstances forced the abandonment of this project.

For the archæologist the country has much of interest. Brochs, stone circles, monoliths, earth-houses, and vitrified forts are numerous, the broch at Dun Dornadilla being the most remarkable of all the Sutherland brochs. The cave of Smoo, near Durness, is a natural and

MACKAY

THE MACKAY BANNER

(By permission of the National Museum of Antiquities of Scotland)

awe-inspiring spectacle. Castles Borve and Varrich are now in ruins, but sufficient of their structure remains to indicate their original strength. Borve, two miles from Farr, is said to have been built by the Norsemen. It became a Mackay stronghold and was destroyed in 1551 following a siege by the Earl of Sutherland. Tongue House was the ancient seat of the chief. In 1656 it was burned down by the forces of the Commonwealth and rebuilt in 1679. Balnakeil, built in 1740, became the chief's second residence. Both are beautiful old houses and Tongue House with its old gardens, green lawns, and sheltering trees, was, to quote an early writer, " a real oasis." Place-names are a combination of Gaelic and Norse, but a large number are pure Norse in their derivation. This is only natural in an area which had been under Norse domination for so many centuries. Tongue was formerly known as Kintail, a Gaelic word meaning " head of the sea." When the parish of Tongue was formed in 1724 the old name was changed, probably to avoid confusion with the other places of the same name. Tongue is derived from the Norse *tung*, meaning a " tongue of land."

Duthaich Mhic Aoidh is rich in traditions of song and poetry. The works of Rob Donn are an outstanding example of the vigour and expression of the poetical traditions of the people. Piping reached a high standard and there have been many famous Mackay pipers. A family of Mackays were hereditary pipers to the Mackenzies of Gairloch from about 1609 to 1805. One of them, Iain Dall (1656–1754), was a friend and pupil of Patrick Og MacCrimmon, and composed much high class pipe music. Angus Mackay was Queen Victoria's piper and was one of the pioneers of the art of putting *piobaireachd* music on paper. Without the scholarly records left by this man, modern knowledge of the classical

B

music of the Highland bagpipe would be fragmentary. There were thirty-six pipers with Mackay's Regiment during the Thirty Years War, but only one had survived when the remnants of the regiment were taken over by Sir John Hepburn in 1634. Kenneth Mackay, a piper in the 79th Highlanders, earned immortal fame by playing the *Piobaireachd, Cogadh no Sith* ("Peace or War"), round the squares between the charges of the French cavalry during the Battle of Waterloo.

The loyalty of the clansmen to their chief has been amply demonstrated by their ready response to his appeals for recruits for his regiments, in which they served him with the same loyalty and courage that they had shown in the many clan battles of earlier years. The Mackay clansmen were a deeply religious people and after the Reformation were much attached to Presbyterianism. During the days of the Episcopacy they held fast to their own form of worship and held field-meetings and conventicles. Lord Reay signed the Covenant, but his attachment to the King caused his loyalty to the Covenant to be suspect. His son, the Master of Reay, later 2nd Lord Reay, assisted the Earl of Huntly, and tried to prevent the men of the Reay country from taking part with the Covenanters. When he became 2nd Lord Reay he assisted in capturing Inverness for the King in 1649 and was for a short time a State prisoner in Edinburgh. He was the only exception when Cromwell released the other State prisoners, but his wife planned and carried out his escape. No Mackays were with the Highland Host ; instead the Mackay country became a refuge for persecuted Covenanters. A detachment of Mackays were present at the Battle of Worcester. From Webster's *Analysis of Population* in 1755, it is learned that all the inhabitants of the Reay country were Protestants.

The organisation inside the clan was much the same as prevailed in other Highland clans. Sub-tenants held their lands from the tacksmen who, in turn, held their lands from the chief. The main estates were Strathnaver, Scourie, Bighouse, Strathy, Melness, and Sandwood. All were in the possession of Mackays, kinsmen of the chief and descended from the main branch. This policy of placing the most valuable and strategic part of his territory in the hands of cadets of the family helped Mackay to knit the whole area into a compact unit, each section helping the other to protect the whole of the clan territory. The Aberach Mackays, who occupied the valley of the Naver, were the oldest cadet. Descended from Ian Aberach, they were known as *Slioc Ean Abrich* and were ever the most fearless section of the clan. They had a reputation for honesty and fair play to their allies. The expression *Ceartas nan Abrich* (" the justice of the Aberachs ") dates from the Battle of Aldicharrish in 1487 when William Du of the Aberach Mackays refused to countenance a MacLeod proposal that the Sutherland men—who had helped them in the battle—should be cheated of their share of the spoil.

II

THE Mackays are of Celtic stock, but the exact identity of the progenitor of the clan has been the subject of much controversy. Genealogical accounts of the family vary with each other, yet are in agreement in assigning a Morayshire origin to the elusive personage who became the founder of the house of Mackay. It is now generally accepted that he descended from the old Royal House of Moray and in all probability the fiery blood of the turbulent McEths ran in his veins. It was long believed that the houses of Mackay and Forbes shared a common ancestor in the person of the great Conachar. The source of this is attributable to Sir Robert Gordon, who, in his *Genealogical History of the Earldom of Sutherland*, traces Mackay's descent from Walter, a natural son of Lord Forbes. This Walter, says Sir Robert, married the daughter of the Bishop of Caithness sometime during the thirteenth century and received from the Bishop twelve davochs of church land at Durness. The tradition of common ancestry was widely believed and both families enjoyed a long and intimate friendship. When Donald, 1st Lord Reay, was raised to the peerage in 1628, he matriculated arms which bore similarity to those of Lord Forbes. He also, on occasion, signed his name " Mackay Forbes," as did his father, an example followed by other prominent Mackay gentlemen. While these points help to indicate the extent of the family friendship, they are insufficient to substantiate claims of common ancestry.

The year 1160 was a momentous one for the Moraymen then thrust from their native province by King Malcolm IV, who gave their lands to his Scoto-Norman followers. The Moraymen scattered throughout the kingdom. Some sought refuge in the Western Isles, others went southward to the lowlands and to Galloway, and many retreated northward to the Province of Cat, then under the sway of the Norsemen. At this time the province included both Caithness and Sutherland. The native Pictish population had been subdued by the Norsemen and had, in all probability, intermarried with their conquerors.

It was a time of change ; the kingdom was slowly being welded into a united nation under one king, and the rebellious Moraymen were feeling the full power of the monarch's growing strength. Foremost of the Moraymen in rebellion against the king was the McEth family.

Their rebellions are too well known to receive more than passing mention. Malcolm McEth, who was the representative of the family at the time of the Moray " Plantation," then held the title of Earl of Ross. In previous years the McEths had been in almost continuous revolt and had carried their disturbances and rebellions as far afield as Galloway. That some of their family or kinsmen settled there is more than likely. In 1296 a Gilmyhel McEthe in Dumfries signed the " Ragman's Roll," and the following year this man is recorded under the name McGethe. The McGhies of Galloway, long regarded as an off-shoot of the Strathnaver Mackays, may have descended from this Gilmyhel McEthe. The Larg Mackies, a section of the Galloway McGhies, received a charter on the thirty pound lands of Cumloden in the Stewartry of Kirkcudbright from King Robert the Bruce. These lands were said to be the Bruce's reward to a widow and her three sons for their assistance to him during the War of Independence. Mackay genealogies credit the foundation of the Galloway McGhies to Martin of Strathnaver but this theory is doubtful. It has also been claimed that the founder of the Strathnaver Mackays was a native of Galloway who came north to assist King William during his campaign against the men of Moray. This Galloway Mackay went to Strathnaver, where he settled and founded the house of Mackay of Strathnaver. There is little evidence to support this claim. The now accepted origin of descent from the Royal House of Moray, through the McEths, is fairly well established.

Malcolm McEth went north after the clearance of Moray and his daughter married Harold, Norse Earl of Caithness. This lady possessed the fiery spirit and rebellious nature of the McEths, and goaded Earl Harold into rebellion against the Scottish king. Harold was killed in battle against the king about 1198, and a tumuli-strewn field at Dalharold in Strathnaver marks the site of this encounter. With the death of Kenneth McEth, in 1214, the McEths slowly disappear from the pages of history. Typical of his race, Kenneth had joined McWilliam's rebellion which King William the Lion subdued after invading Strathnaver. Following Kenneth's death, the Mackays begin to emerge from the opaque past.

The church lands at Durness were owned by the Mackays from an early date, but whether the first occupier of them was the Bishop's son-in-law or grandson is uncertain. Doubts and uncertainties regarding individual Mackays disappear with the advent of Iye Mackay, chief from about 1330 to 1370. The mother of this Iye was a daughter of Iye of Gigha, and from this time the genealogy of the Strathnaver family is on sure ground.

A family of Mackays in Argyll held prominent positions and offices under the Lord of the Isles and, like the Galloway McGhies, are claimed to have descended from the Strathnaver family. In 1329 King Robert the Bruce gave lands in Kintyre to Gilchrist macYmar McCay for the service of two bowmen in the king's army. The famous Gaelic charter of 1408 by MacDonald of the Isles conferred on Brian Vicar Mackay lands in Islay. The charter from the Bruce is interesting and tends to confirm the early services of Mackays to the Crown during the Scottish War of Independence. It has long been accepted that Mackays formed part of the Scottish army at the Battle of Bannockburn and it is probable that all three branches were present. Historians, in the absence of proof, are doubtful if the Strathnaver Mackays were with the northern clans who fought at Bannockburn, but they are inclined to believe that the Mackays would, in all probability, have joined the Highland supporters of the Bruce.

It is questionable if the Argyll Mackays can be claimed as a branch of the House of Strathnaver. It has been argued that they are of the same kin, either (a) through a McEth who settled in Argyll after the Moray episode of 1160, or (b) through an unnamed Strathnaver Mackay who settled in Argyll at an early date. The Bruce's charter clearly shows that the Argyll Mackays had reached some prominence by 1329. The name *Aodh* was a favourite with the Celtic people, and in the Celtic district of Argyll it was common in its forms of *Aodh*, *Y*, and *Iye*. Even assuming that the Argyll Mackays like the Mackays of Strathnaver descended from some-one named *Aodh*, there is little proof that the same *Aodh* was the progenitor of both houses. In the Gaelic MS. of 1450 a Clan Aid (*Aoidh*) is listed, but the genealogical details probably relate to the Argyll branch and not to the main Strathnaver family.

The history of the Mackays of Strathnaver is a long record of conflict and warfare. During four centuries they were involved in almost continuous fighting, mainly against their neighbours. The House of Sutherland was their most bitter and relentless foe, but the Gunns, Sinclairs, and MacLeods whose lands adjoined *Duthaich Mhic Aoidh* never lost an opportunity of invading Strath-naver. The Earl of Sutherland claimed superiority over Mackay, a claim bitterly resented and resisted by succes-sive Mackay chiefs. In 1583 Sutherland obtained the superiority of Strathnaver from the Earl of Huntly and thereafter regarded Mackay as his chief vassal. Such were the conditions of the times that Mackay was able to resist Sutherland's claims. Huisdean Du, chief from 1572–1612, had, like his ancestors, refused to acknowledge Sutherland's superiority, but eventually,

in circumstances which will be explained later, he accepted
Sutherland as his superior.

A factor which contributed greatly to Mackay's
troubles was the allodial or independent possession of
his estate. It was not until 1499 that he obtained a
charter for his lands. Hitherto, the sword had been
sufficient protection against invading enemies, but, as
times changed, the possession of a charter had greater
value than weight of arms.

Even as early as 1370, Iye Mackay was involved in
intermittent disputes with the Earl of Sutherland. At
this time the Mackays were looked upon by the Earl as
" ancient enemies," a term which suggests that the
Mackays were not newcomers to Strathnaver. The
dispute between both parties appears to have come to a
head in 1370, and in an effort to bring peace between
them and to adjust their differences a meeting was
arranged at Dingwall with umpires to decide the issue.
Mackay, or so we are told, was on the point of proving
his claim when Sutherland murdered him and his son
and heir. After this act of treacherous brutality Sutherland fled home pursued by Mackay's retainers and the
feud between them grew more bitter and intense. It
may well be that the dispute arose from Sutherland's
claim of superiority over Strathnaver. Married to King
David II's sister, he had received the Earldom of Sutherland in regality in 1345. The grant of regality settled the
succession on the lawful heirs of the Earl and the King's
sister, but the only child of this union predeceased his
father, and, or so the Mackays argued, the heirs of the
Earl's second marriage were not legally entitled to the
regality. Sutherland, however, refused to relinquish
claims over Mackay and prosecuted them with relentless
vigour.

III

THE pattern of Mackay history must be viewed against a background of almost never-ending strife. It had the two-fold purpose of opposition to the claims of superiority over them, and determination to protect and preserve their ancestral territory from the invasions and depredations of their neighbours.

The military ability and fighting qualities of the Mackays have never been doubted, but the same cannot be said of their diplomacy. They were slow to take advantage of changing conditions which placed greater value upon the possession of a legal charter for their lands than upon the power of the sword to retain them. Sir Robert Gordon, sometimes referred to as " the father of Highland History," deals very extensively with the Mackay and Sutherland history in his *Genealogical History of the Earldom of Sutherland*. Many of Sir Robert's statements, however, must be treated with caution. His purpose was to uphold the House of Sutherland and he never missed an opportunity to belittle Mackay. Yet his work is invaluable in that it gives an excellent all-over picture of the Highland scene—its battles, intrigues, and politics. The Mackay histories, quite naturally, treat Mackay–Sutherland differences from the Mackay viewpoint, and they conflict with Sir Robert's work in many important details. The interested reader, however, will find perusal of the many charters and papers of both families of great value and from them can draw his own conclusions.

There were three distinct periods in Mackay history. The first brings us to the end of the sixteenth century and was a period of continuous warfare in the protection

C

of their possessions. The second period carries us to the beginning of the nineteenth century—it witnessed the climax of Mackay power and influence and the achievement of great military honour and glory by the Mackay regiments, but it also ushered in the beginning of Mackay financial difficulties which forced the sale of parts of *Duthaich Mhic Aoidh* to the House of Sutherland. The final period may be called the swan song of the Mackays. The last of the Mackay country was sold and the Sutherland clearances swept from the glens and straths the descendants of those who had so valiantly defended the country of Mackay.

Clan feuds were common in the Highlands, but no clan was ever engaged in such long and bitter fighting as were the Mackays. During four centuries they fought battle after battle ; and as battles are not fought without casualties, the Mackays must have been numerically strong to withstand such a constant drain upon their manpower. In 1411 the Lord of the Isles in his campaign to seize the Earldom of Ross was opposed at Dingwall by Mackay at the head of an army composed of Mackays, Rosses, Munros, and Sutherlands. Mackay was in command of this joint force, a fact which suggests that, at that time, he was the most powerful chief in the north. When Angus Du answered King James I's summons to attend the Inverness Parliament of 1428, he was described as " a leader of 4,000 men." At the time of the Jacobite Rebellion of 1745-46 the Mackay strength was placed at 800 fighting men. The Mackays fought at least ten pitched battles between 1400 and 1550, most of them against those who had invaded Strathnaver. It must not be supposed that the Mackays spent all their time protecting themselves. Far from it ! Whenever the opportunity arose they indulged in foraging raids on Sutherland, Caithness, and Ross. " An eye for an eye " was the order of the day, and in this the Mackays were no better or no worse than other Highland clans. Highland pride demanded that no insult be overlooked and that attack must be met by counter-attack.

It was inevitable that acts of violence should have been committed during the disturbed period of clan warfare, and even the sanctity of the Church was violated. When Thomas Mackay pursued Mowatt of Caithness—with whom he had a dispute—to Tain, he killed Mowatt and burned St. Duthus Chapel where Mowatt's men had taken refuge. During a Mackay invasion of Navidale, the chapel of St. Ninian was set on fire, and even Dornoch Cathedral was burned at the hands of Mackay and the Master of Caithness.

The preoccupation of the Mackays with affairs at home did not prevent them from acting in the service of the Crown. On several occasions they carried out commissions against other Highland clans, not the least of which was against the outlawed Torquil MacLeod of the Lews. Iye Roy Mackay was present at the siege of Stornoway Castle in 1506 when Torquil was captured. In reward for his services the King gave Mackay the non-entry of the lands of Strathnaver, Strathhalladale, Creichmore, Assynt, Coigach, etc., in 1506. Mackay and his brother were present at the Battle of Flodden, and Mackays were also present at Solway Moss. In this encounter, Iye Du, son of the chief, was taken prisoner and sent captive to England. While there, along with some of his fellow countrymen, also prisoners, he acquiesced to the scheme of King Henry VIII to unite the two nations by the marriage of Edward of England and the infant Queen Mary of Scots. Iye Du took part in the attack on Arran at Glasgow in 1543, and thereafter, returning to England, he served in the military forces

of that country for a few years. While in England he
gained considerable military experience which stood
him in good stead when he returned to Strathnaver.
He attended Mary, Queen of Scots, when she visited
Inverness in 1562, and received a remission from the
Queen for his previous crimes. Had he taken the
opportunity at this time of obtaining the renewal of his
father's charters, Mackay history might have taken
another course. Some years later, charges of bastardy
were levied against him, his lands escheated and given
to the Earl of Huntly. Unable to take possession of
Strathnaver, Huntly was glad to sell the lands to Mackay,
but Huntly retained the feudal superiority which he
afterwards granted to the Earl of Sutherland.

During the minority of Iye Du's son, Huisdean, we
find the first serious breach in Mackay unity. Huisdean
was a minor and the ward of the Earl of Caithness. His
two elder half-brothers were debarred from the chiefship
on the plea that they were illegitimate, their mother
being the hand-fasted wife of Iye Du. The elder, Donald
Balloch, became the founder of the Scourie branch.
The Aberach Mackays were friendly to Donald Balloch,
who had been brought up with them at Achness, and
favoured him as chief. The Earl of Caithness, to suit
his own purpose, sowed dissension amongst the Mackays
and their allies, so that the clan, for the first time in its
history, was divided against itself. The Aberach Mackays
withdrew their support from their chief and allied themselves with Sutherland. The defection of his most
numerous branch, whose loyalty and courage in battle
had been the cornerstone of Mackay strength, was a
severe handicap to young Huisdean Du when he took
up the reins of chiefship. Between his kinsmen, the
Earl of Caithness and the Earl of Sutherland, both of
whom were anxious to encompass his ruin, he was in a

sorry position. Huisdean Du settled the lands of Scourie on Donald Balloch, but failed to give the Aberachs title to Strathnaver which they held in life-rent. Had Huisdean Du used tact at this time, he might have reunited his clan and saved himself many of the misfortunes which later befell him. Anxious to have Mackay as an ally, Sutherland made a proposal to Huisdean Du —the non-entry dues on Mackay's lands amounting to £50,000 Scots would be cancelled and Sutherland's daughter given to him in marriage if Mackay acknowledged Sutherland's feudal superiority. Mackay agreed.

A prophecy, attributable to the Red Friar (*Sagard Ruadh*), was then widely believed and foretold the downfall and ruin of the House of Mackay when a chief married into the House of Sutherland. The Red Priest of Strathnaver is sometimes identified as St. Maelrubha who, tradition claims, was martyred in Strathnaver by the Danes, *circa* A.D. 723. Earlier chiefs had married into the prominent Highland families of MacDonald, Fraser, Cameron, Mackintosh, MacKenzie, and Munro, to name but a few. It cannot, however, be claimed that these unions furthered Mackay interests. The battle of Tuthim-Tarbach, fought in the late fourteenth century between the Mackays and the MacLeods, occurred as a result of a dispute between the tutor of Mackay and his MacLeod sister-in-law. This battle between the two families proves to some extent the unreliability of Highland marriage relationships in furthering ties of friendship. Marriage into the Ross of Balnagown family was equally unproductive. Angus Mackay of Strathnaver, whose mother was a Ross of Balnagown, invaded Ross and was driven into the church at Tarbat and killed. The Mackays revenged this action at Aldicharrich. Highland politics were too involved and uncertain to permit inter-clan marriages to affect the trend of events. Bonds of friendship, except with old and trusted friends, seldom lasted and were only temporary or short-lived at best. Several times Mackay chiefs married their cousins or near kin, such unions being illegal unless Papal dispensation was first obtained. They also married by hand-fasting, a system whereby both parties agreed to live together for a year, and if at the end of that period an heir was born, the marriage was accepted as binding without further ceremony. Such unions brought charges of illegitimacy against the Mackays and involved them in considerable trouble, endangering the succession to, and ownership of, their lands.

Superstition apart, it was during the chiefship of the child of this union between Mackay and Sutherland that the Mackays reached new fame for their military prowess.

IV

Donald Mackay, who became Sir Donald Mackay of Farr and later Lord Reay, won for himself a high reputation for bravery and leadership. In his younger days he had concerned himself with the management of his estates and added to them by purchase. In 1626, hoping to advance his fortunes, he raised a regiment for service in the Protestant cause during the Thirty Years War. Mackay's Regiment was recruited mainly in the County of Sutherland, and of the first 3,000 recruits the majority were men from Mackay's own territory. The story of the regiment's service, its exploits and feats of valour, has been faithfully recorded by Munro in his *Expedition*, published in 1637 and one of the earliest printed British military records. The defence of the Pass of Oldenberg was one of the finest feats of this gallant regiment. It is not surprising that Lord Reay sought to perpetuate the memory of his regiment by including the figures of two musketeers as supporters in his Coat of Arms. After serving under the King of Denmark and Gustavus Adolphus, King of Sweden, the remnants of the regiment were taken over by Sir John Hepburn.

Mackay, who, in all, had recruited 10,000 men, was raised to the Scottish Peerage in 1628 as Lord Reay. He had incurred heavy financial commitments, and after the death of Gustavus Adolphus there was little hope of reimbursement. Involved in political affairs at home and with matrimonial troubles adding to his worries, Lord Reay was in a desperate position. His loyalty and service to King Charles I made him suspect by the Covenanters, and he was looked upon with disfavour by the Privy Council. He disposed of part of his estates to pay his debts, and Strathnaver, home of the Aberach branch, became the property of the Earl of Sutherland. Lord Reay died in Denmark in 1649, and was buried in the family vault at Kirkiboll. He was a real Mackay in that he possessed the spirit and fighting qualities of his ancestors, but he also displayed a lack of tact and diplomacy—qualities as necessary as courage in the troubled times in which he lived.

Mackays served with the " Scots Brigade " in Holland, and General Hugh Mackay, of the Scourie branch, rose to the command of the whole Scots Brigade. In 1688 he brought the Brigade over to Britain and, as Commander-in-Chief in Scotland, was mainly responsible for the pacification of the country, a duty which he carried out with the utmost skill and leadership. He commanded the Government forces at the Battle of Killiecrankie in 1689, in which engagement a large number of

Mackays served under him. General Mackay has always been held in high esteem, not only for his military leadership but also for his clemency to the vanquished.

While not quite so famous as " Mackay's Regiment," the " Reay Fencibles," 1794–1802, served with distinction in Ireland. General Lake had the utmost confidence in them, as can be seen from his high tribute to them after his defeat at Castlebar : " If I had my brave and honest Reays with me, this would not have happened." Their victory at Tara Hill was an outstanding achievement.

During the Jacobite Rebellions of 1715 and 1745–46, the Mackays remained loyal to the Government. In his *The Highlanders of Scotland*, W. F. Skene bitterly criticised Clan Mackay for their loyalty to the Hanoverian monarch. He attributes Lord Reay's support of the Government to have been activated by a desire to retain his peerage which had been bestowed on his ancestor by a Stewart monarch. Skene's criticism is unjust in that it might equally have been said of other loyal clans. The services given by Mackays to the Stewart monarchs had been ill-rewarded and were largely responsible for the financial difficulties of the 1st Lord Reay. George, 3rd Lord Reay, chief from 1680–1748, was a man of outstanding character and for 30 years devoted himself to the religious and educational welfare of his people, who held him in esteem as Am Morair Mor (the great lord). He was a staunch Protestant and politically and temperamentally opposed to any change of regime which might affect the religious life of the nation. He did not succumb to the sentiment which swept so many others into the maelstrom of civil war in support of the Jacobites, and thereby, to some extent, he protected his people from the miseries and hardships which followed the defeat of the Rebels.

In 1715 the Mackays took up arms for King George I and helped to prevent the Northern Highland Clans joining the Jacobites. In company with the Frasers, Munros, Rosses, and Sutherlands, they assisted in capturing from the Jacobites the town and castle of Inverness, which they garrisoned for some time after the suppression of the Rebellion. When the second Jacobite Rebellion took place, George, 3rd Lord Reay, had no hesitation in supporting the Government. Mackays served in Lord Loudon's regiment and guarded Inverness and other places north of the Spey. A party of Mackays were responsible for the capture of the Jacobite Earl of Cromartie who had sought refuge in Dunrobin Castle. While the clan as a body remained loyal to the Government, individual Mackays, mainly from outside the clan country, took up arms on behalf of Prince Charles Edward. From 1745 onwards, the history of the Mackays is a record of their military service in the armed forces of the Crown. In the three Sutherland Fencibles, Mackays served with distinction. Rob Donn, the Reay Bard, served with the 1st Sutherland Fencibles raised in 1759. He was more a regimental bard than a soldier.

V

THE social and economic changes of the nineteenth century did not bring peace and prosperity to the people of the Reay country. The century had hardly begun when the first clearance took place. Prior to 1806 there had been partial removals from Lord Reay's estates when he reduced the leases of tenants. Of these removals we are told they " . . . were under ordinary and comparatively favourable circumstances. Those who were ejected from their farms were accommodated

D

with smaller portions of land. . . ." It is the " Sutherland Clearances " which have aroused so much bitter controversy. Both the Countess of Sutherland and her husband, the Marquis of Stafford, were genuinely anxious to improve the Sutherland estates and spent over £200,000 on buildings, communications and land improvement, for which they got little in the way of increased rents. They were, however, mistaken in trying to thrust up-to-date methods too quickly on a backward population ; their transference of tenants from the interior to the coast became economically disastrous when the kelp industry failed and inshore fisheries declined ; and they were unfortunate in their choice of agents. The methods used in carrying out the clearances were brutal and odious. In his *Gloomy Memories* Donald MacLeod gives a graphic account of the Sutherland clearances, and the details of the hardship and suffering of the evicted tenants make dismal reading. While, at times, the author may be guilty of over-emphasis, his accusations were only too well-founded, and are substantially confirmed by the Rev. Donald Sage, minister at Achness, in his *Memorabilia Domestica*. *Duthaich Mhic Aoidh*, the greater part of which was then in the possession of the Countess of Sutherland, suffered more from the evictions than any other part of the country. Strathnaver was almost completely denuded of its inhabitants, descendants of those Aberachs who had so faithfully served successive Mackay chiefs.

In 1829 Eric, 7th Lord Reay, sold the last of his estate to the Marquis of Stafford, afterwards Duke of Sutherland, and *Duthaich Mhic Aoidh* became the property of the clan's oldest antagonist. The price paid was £300,000, and its annual rental value was just over £10,000. Absorbed into the Sutherland estate, the " Country of Mackay " became a misnomer. Not one acre of land was retained by the chief or his cadet families. At the time of writing, the position is unchanged, neither Lord Reay nor his cadets owning any land within the ancient clan country.

Thus the ancient patrimony of the clan which had been so valiantly defended and zealously guarded during five centuries was lost through the extravagance of an absentee chief. The lands of Durness which constituted the first Mackay possessions in the north were the last to be sold.

A critic of the clan has said that the tragedy of Mackay was two-fold, their passion for following lost causes and their loyalty. There is an element of truth in this statement. The progenitor of Mackay was descended from a follower of the lost cause of the Men of Moray, and both the 1st and 2nd Lord Reay followed the " lost cause " of the Episcopacy. Of their loyalty it can be said that, once given, it was unswerving. After the accession of the House of Hanover, they transferred their loyalty to the Crown, probably for religious motives. They were too honest to engage in subterfuge at a time when this was the only means of advancing their own interests. They relied more upon the sword than upon the security of a legal charter. They dissipated their strength in battles which gained them only temporary and local advantage.

On the death of Eric, 9th Lord Reay, in 1875, the succession passed to the Dutch branch of the family, descendants of Æneas Mackay, son of the 2nd Lord Reay. This notable family had risen to prominence in the country of their adoption ; the first Dutch holder of the title of Lord Reay was a Baron of the Netherlands and Vice-President of the Council of State. His son, the 11th Lord Reay, was naturalised in 1877 and created Baron Reay of Durness in the Peerage of the United Kingdom

in 1881. He died in 1921, when the United Kingdom
Peerage became extinct, and was succeeded in his
Scottish title by his cousin Baron Eric, 12th Lord Reay.

The late chief, Æneas Alexander, 13th Lord Reay,
baronet of Nova Scotia and Baron Mackay of Ophemert,
in Holland, succeeded his father in 1921. On the 19th
July, 1924, Lord Reay was invested as Chief of Clan
Mackay at Reay, in presence of a large gathering of
clansmen. The Chief was presented with a parchment
of investiture and a silver box containing soil and pebbles
taken from the ground of title.

The 13th Lord Reay, who died in Kenya, was
married and had a son and two daughters. His son,
Hugh William Mackay, born in 1937, succeeded to the
title as 14th Lord Reay in 1963. He is married and his
son and heir, Aeneas Simon Mackay was born in 1965.

Clan Music

Bratach Bhan Chloinn Aoidh or the Mackays' White Banner

The composer of this fine old Gathering, said to be one of the finest in
existence, is unknown. Angus Mackay noted in 1829 that " The White
Flag " was very ancient and that it was then in existence.

Iseabal Nic Aoidh or Isabel Mackay

The composer of this salute is unknown but the tune was written in
honour of Isabel Mackay, daughter of John Mackay (1685–1753), second
son of Hector Mackay of Skerray. A song, which is usually sung to the
air of " The Prince's Salute," was also composed in honour of this lady by
Rob Donn.

Chloinn Aoidh, or The Mackays' March

This March has long been regarded by Mackays as clan music, but in
early collections it is recorded under the names " Chisholm of Strathglass's
Salute " and as " Chisholm's March." In his manuscript Angus Mackay
recorded it but did not name it. Later he added the words " The Mackay
March," in pencil.

Cumha Dhomhunill Dhuaghal Mhic Aoidh, or Lament for Donald Mackay, 1st Lord Reay

This composition is attributed to Donald Mor MacCrimmon.

A pipe tune called " Lord Reay's Fencibles " was composed either during or shortly after the regiment's period of service. The composer is unknown. "Am Priosaneachadh encorach" (*the unjust incarceration*) was composed by John Dall Mackay (1666–1754), hereditary piper to the Mackenzies of Gairloch. The tune is said to commemorate the imprisonment of Neil Vass, son of Angus Du, who was sent as a hostage to the Bass Rock in 1427.

Pipe tunes and other music connected with the clan will be found in Captain Fraser of Knockie's Collection of Highland Music and the David Glen Collection.

Names said by some authorities to be associated with Clan Mackay

Bain	Macghie	Macquoid	Polson
Bayne	Mackee	Macvail	Scobie
MacCay	Mackie	Morgan	Williamson
MacCrie	MacPhail	Neilson	
Macghee	Macquey	Paul	

Miscellaneous Clan Notes

Name

The surname Mackay is the English equivalent of the Gaelic *MacAoidh* from *Mac* (son) and *Aoidh* (the genitive of the proper name *Aodh*). *Aodh* was a popular Celtic name and is said to be a form of *Aed* which is translated as " The fiery or impetuous one." With the passing of time, the spelling of *MacAoidh* has taken many forms including Iye, Y, Aytho, MacIye, Makky, Macky, Maky, McKye, McKeye, Mackie, Mackey, McKy, McAy, McCei, MacCay, Mackee, Makgie, Ison, Eason, Easson, and many others. The name MacIsaac is said to be a corruption of MacIye. Clan Morgan, the old name for Clan Mackay, may be derived from the Moray connection of the clan. Earliest reference to Clan Morgan is found in the *Book of Deer*, where the toisheach of the clan is so described. Sir Robert Gordon tells us that the clan was termed Clan-Vic-Morgan from one Morgan who flourished in the fourteenth century.

Slogan

" *Bratach Bhan Chlann Aoidh* " (The White Banner of Mackay).

Badge

Reed grass, great bulrush, broom.

The great bulrush has been officially recorded in Lyon Office as the badge. Reed grass (Gaelic, *Cuilc*) has long been regarded by clansmen as the true badge. *Cuilc* grows freely in the Reay country and its thick stems were used in the making of bagpipe reeds.

Mackay Banner

There has been much controversy regarding this banner which is claimed to be the *Bratach Bhan Chlann Aoidh*. It is now in the Scottish National Museum of Antiquities where it was placed for safe-keeping by the Clan Mackay Society. For many years it was in the possession of an Aberach Mackay known as Huistean na Bratach (Hugh of the Banner) and was claimed to have been the battle flag of Ian Aberach (progenitor of the Aberach Mackays) who led the clan at the battle of Drum na coup in 1433. The banner measures 30 inches by 16 inches and is of faded cream-white silk. Within a double tressured shield is the outline of a lion rampant in blue with fleurs-de-lis, and above a hand-like object outlined in gold-coloured thread with blue bars across the wrist and the words " Be Tren " across the palm. Around is the legend " Verk visly and Tent to ye end." The illustration shows the banner to be the work of someone unacquainted with heraldry. The leather attachment for the hoist, which may be a replacement, occupies a position on one of the short sides of the banner, which, if flown, would place the lion shield on its side. No doubt the hoist was originally on one of the long sides, thus the banner, when displayed, would have the shield in the correct position. The size of the banner would suggest that part only has been preserved of what may originally have been a much larger flag.

The arms of Mackay of Strathnaver in 1503 were three stars and a hand erased, appaumé. These were the arms of the Mackay chiefs until the family was ennobled in 1628. It is extremely doubtful if the banner is as old as is claimed. Expert opinion dates it from the late sixteenth century or early seventeenth century. There is little doubt it is an old Mackay banner which may have come into the possession of the Aberach branch after the 1st Lord Reay adopted other arms. The banner has long been known as the White Banner of Mackay and has been traditionally accepted as such. Sir Robert Gordon, in his letter of advice to his nephew, the Earl of Sutherland, written about 1626-27, said : " Let Mckay, his pincell never be displayed where yours is, whether you be personally present or some other having your place, let him have his pincell folded up when yours is displayed." This may be interpreted as either a continuation of the Sutherland claim to superiority over Mackay, or as an attempt to suppress the Mackay banner, or as both.

It has sometimes been claimed that the Mackay banner is really the banner of the Grays who were hereditary constables of Skibo Castle. In 1740 Lieutenant Robert Gray of Skibo was involved in a dispute with his two half-sisters and his brother-in-law, John Mackay of Tordarroch. Gray raised a process for the recovery of certain family papers and for the constables' banner, which, it was alleged, had been taken away by a

Mackay. The banner of the hereditary constable of Skibo bore the armorial bearing of the Gray family, namely : a lion rampant within a bordure engrailed charged with eight thistles, within a shield ; crest—an arm erect grasping a heart ; motto—" Constable."

The first extant written mention of the Mackay banner appears in the first *Statistical Account* (1791–99) when it was recorded as being in the possession of an Aberach Mackay. Had there been any doubts regarding the banner or any tradition of it belonging to the Grays, we venture to suggest that the writer of the *Statistical Account* would have recorded it.

Tartan

The tartan of Clan Mackay illustrated here is a simple arrangement of three colours and bears resemblance to the Gunn and the Morrison tartans. It has been claimed, and it may well be, that the Mackay tartan was originally a district pattern. The Gunns and Morrisons were allies of Mackay. The writer has in her possession a fragment of hard spun Mackay tartan, in light colour shades, taken from a plaid worn by an officer in the Reay Fencibles (1794–1802). The tartan for this regiment was supplied by Messrs. William Wilson and Sons, Bannockburn. In the pattern book of Messrs. Bolingbroke and Jones, Norwich, there is a Mackay pattern with a yellow overstripe. It is somewhat similar to the Campbell of Breadalbane tartan. In Inverness Museum there is a tartan coat, period *circa* late eighteenth century, which, until recently, was in the possession of a Strathnaver Mackay whose ancestor wore it as Mackay tartan. The design is that of the Campbell of Breadalbane with brown instead of black, but with the yellow overstripe in the same position as in the Breadalbane. It is possible the brown colour may be faded black. In the *Vestiarium Scoticum*, published in 1842, the authors illustrate a Mackay tartan in blue and black colours with a red overstripe. This has never been accepted as a true Mackay tartan. During the past few years a tweed-like design called " Mackay of Strathnaver tartan " has become popular. Its history is obscure but is claimed to have been copied from a plaid taken to America by a Mackay from Strathnaver in the early nineteenth century. Some members of the clan wear this as a hunting tartan.

In a contemporary account of the Mackay Regiment formed in 1626 it is stated that the men wore Highland dress with kilts of dark green tartan. This regiment was the first regularly organised military unit to have Highland dress as its uniform. In October 1751, John Mackay, described as " of Rosshall in the County of Strathnaver," was arrested in Inverness and charged with wearing a tartan coat and plaid, the wearing of tartan being then prohibited. He was sentenced to six months' imprisonment.

Clan Society

In 1806 a " Mackay's Society " was formed in Glasgow ; it is the oldest Clan Society now in existence. From the rules of the Society it is clear that its formation was more that of a benevolent and funeral society than that of a present-day Clan Association. In 1888 it was reconstituted as " The Clan Mackay Society," and has branches in Glasgow, Edinburgh,

London, and overseas. Membership is open to all persons surnamed Mackay and MacAoidh. Holders of surnames recognised as Sept names may be accepted as associates.

Non-entry and non-entry dues

Both are old Scottish legal terms connected with the feudal system of land tenure.

Originally, the Crown was the universal landowner from whom Crown vassals held their lands in return for services and/or other payments to the Crown. The Crown vassals sub-feued parts of their lands in return for services to themselves and the sub-feuers became vassals of their " superior," the Crown vassal.

The Mackays originally held their lands as allodial possessions or as land outside the feudal system. In 1499 a Crown charter was obtained and the Mackay lands were henceforth held under feudal possession.

Under the feudal system every heir had, on the death of the holder, to enter himself as legal heir and renew his investiture with his superior. Failure to comply with this legal obligation was called " non-entry," indicating that no legal heir was in possession of them. Failure of an heir to renew investiture involved payment to his land superior of a feudal casualty or fine which was called " non-entry dues " or " casualties."

Bibliography

The undernoted is a selection of sources of information available on the history of the clan. Further references will be found in *Scottish Family History* by Stuart and Balfour Paul, published by Oliver and Boyd in 1930.

History of the House and Clan of Mackay, by Robert Mackay, 1829.

The Book of Mackay, by Rev. Angus Mackay, 1906.

An Old Scots Brigade, being the History of Mackay's Regiment now incorporated with the Royal Scots, by John Mackay, 1885.

Genealogical History of the Earldom of Sutherland, by Sir Robert Gordon, edited by John Loch, 1813.

History of the Province of Cat (Caithness and Sutherland), by the Rev. Angus Mackay, 1914.

Sutherland and the Reay Country, by the Rev. A. Gunn and John Mackay, 1897.

The Reay Fencibles or Lord Reay's Highlanders, by John Mackay, 1890.

An Old Highland Fencible Corps (The History of the Reay Fencibles Regiment of Foot) Mackay's Regiment, 1794–1802, by I. H. Mackay-Scobie, 1914.

Life of General Hugh Mackay of Scourie, by John Mackay, 1836.

Monro, His Expedition with the Worthy Scots Regiment (Called Mac-Keyes Regiment), 1637.

Chief of Mackay, by Ian Grimble, 1965.